After the

Dennis K

methuen | drama

LONDON • NEW YORK • OXFORD • NEW DELHI • SYDNEY

METHUEN DRAMA
Bloomsbury Publishing Plc
50 Bedford Square, London, WC1B 3DP, UK
1385 Broadway, New York, NY 10018, USA
29 Earlsfort Terrace, Dublin 2, Ireland

BLOOMSBURY, METHUEN DRAMA and the Methuen Drama logo are trademarks of Bloomsbury Publishing Plc

First published in Great Britain 2005

This edition published 2022

Cover design: Jade Barnett

Cover image © Penique Productions

A catalogue record for this book is available from the British Library.

Library of Congress Control Number: 2022932018

ISBN: PB: 978-1-3503-3921-7
ePDF: 978-1-3503-3922-4
eBook: 978-1-3503-3923-1

Series: Modern Plays

Typeset by Mark Heslington Ltd, Scarborough, North Yorkshire
Printed and bound in Great Britain

To find out more about our authors and books visit www.bloomsbury.com and sign up for our newsletters.

STRATFORD EAST

A THEATRE ROYAL STRATFORD EAST PRODUCTION

AFTER THE END

By Dennis Kelly

After The End was first produced by Paines Plough Theatre Company at the Traverse Theatre on 5 August 2005 and subsequently at the Bush Theatre, London

VAT NO:233 3120 59 | CHARITY REG. NO: 233801 | REG. NO: 556251
Theatre Royal Stratford East, Gerry Raffles Square, London E15 1BN
www.stratfordeast.com

CAST

Mark	**Nick Blood**
Louise	**Amaka Okafor**

Performed at Theatre Royal Stratford East

25 February–26 March 2022

CREATIVE TEAM

Written by	Dennis Kelly
Directed by	Lyndsey Turner
Designer	Peter McKintosh
Lighting Designer	Tim Lutkin
Sound Designer & Composer	Tingying Dong
Sound Design Mentor	Paul Arditti
Design Associate	Alice Hallifax
Assistant Director	Aaliyah McKay
Fight Director	Bret Yount
Casting Director	Isabella Odoffin
Casting Assistant	Joanna Sturrock

PRODUCTION TEAM

Production Manager	Ben Arkell
Stage Manager	Chris Peterson
Stage Manager (on the book)	Anna Sheard
Costume Supervisor	Fiona Parker
Props Supervisor	Propworks/Kate Dowling
Scenic Art	Richard Nutbourne
Head of Production	Jess Harwood
Head of Stage	Dominic Kelly
Stage Deputy	Daniel Steward
Head of LX	Deanna Towli
Senior Technician Lighting & Video	Jamie Haigh
Head of Sound	Jeremy George
Production & Events Technician	Ross Monteiro

Set built by Theatre Royal Stratford East Workshop

Thank You to:

Young Vic

Nick Blood (Mark)

Nick was most recently seen starring in Michael Samuel's Channel 4 drama *Close to Me*, opposite Connie Neilsen and Christopher Eccleston. In 2021 he performed the lead role in the independent film *Abyzou* before going straight on to play a role in the Untitled Disney Plus series. Straight after this he started shooting on another feature film, *Lovely, Dark & Deep*, opposite Georgina Campbell. Other notable screen work includes the independent feature *Body of Water*, opposite Sian Brook. Other recent screen credits include HBO's *Euphoria*, *Lethal White*, Danny Boyle's *Babylon*, *Misfits* and *Him & Her*, but he is perhaps best known for his role as mercenary Lance Hunter in Marvel's *Agents of S.H.I.E.L.D.* His stage career began as Adam in *The Priory* (Royal Court), followed by Marianne Elliott's production of *Women Beware Women* (National Theatre). He later played the major role of Stuart Sutcliffe ('the fifth Beatle') in the West End production of *Backbeat*, which also took him to Toronto and Los Angeles.

Amaka Okafor (Louise)

Theatre credits include *Nora: A Doll's House* (Young Vic), *The Son* (Kiln Theatre and West End), *I'm Not Running*, *Macbeth*, *Saint George and the Dragon*, *Peter Pan* (National Theatre), *Hamlet* (Almeida Theatre), *Grimly Handsome*, *I See You* (Royal Court), *Hamlet* (Barbican), *Glasgow Girls* (Citizen Theatre), *Dr Korczak's Example* (Manchester Royal Exchange & Arcola) and *The Bacchae* (National Theatre of Scotland). Her television credits include *The Responder*, *Grace*, *Des*, *The Split Series 2*, *Vera* and film credits include *Sweet Sue*.

Dennis Kelly (Writer)

Work for theatre includes *Debris, Osama the Hero, After the End, Love and Money, Taking Care of Baby, DNA, Orphans, The Gods Weep, The Ritual Slaughter of Gorge Mastromas, Girls and Boys* and *The Regression.* For television, he has written and created *Utopia, Pulling* (co-written, co-created), *The Third Day* (co-created) and *Together*, and for film he wrote the screenplay for *Black Sea.* He also wrote the book for the Olivier and Tony Award-winning *Matilda: The Musical* and in 2010 *DNA* became a set text on the GCSE English Literature syllabus.

Lyndsey Turner (Director)

Previous directing work includes *Noye's Fludde* (Theatre Royal Stratford East), *Top Girls, Saint George and the Dragon, Light Shining in Buckinghamshire, Edgar and Annabel, There Is a War* (National Theatre), *Girls and Boys* (Royal Court), *Hamlet* (Barbican), *Chimerica* (Almeida & West End), *Aristocrats, Philadelphia, Here I Come!, Fathers and Sons* and *Faith Healer* (Donmar).

Peter McKintosh (Designer)

Peter is a Tony and Olivier Award-nominated designer. He won the Olivier Award for Best Costume Design for *Crazy for You* (Regent's Park/Novello).

Theatre credits include *Shining City, Extinct, The Sun, The Moon and the Stars, King Hedley II* (Theatre Royal Stratford East), *South Pacific* (Chichester & UK tour), *Twelve Angry Men* (Tokyo), *Funny Girl, Guys and Dolls* (Marigny, Paris), *42nd Street* (Châtelet, Paris), *The Winslow Boy* (Old Vic/New York), *A Day in the Death of Joe Egg, The Wind in the Willows, Guys and Dolls, Dirty Rotten Scoundrels, My Night with Reg, Hay Fever, Fiddler on the Roof, Entertaining Mr Sloane, The Dumb Waiter, Viva Forever!, Noises Off, Love Story, Donkeys' Years, The Birthday Party* (West End), *The 39 Steps*

(London, New York and worldwide; Tony Award nominations for Best Scenic and Best Costume Design), *Our Country's Good, The Doctor's Dilemma, Widowers' Houses, Honk!* (National Theatre), *Pericles, King John, The Merry Wives of Windsor, Brand* (RSC), *The York Realist, Arturo Ui, Luise Miller, The Chalk Garden, John Gabriel Borkman, The Cryptogram* (Donmar) and *On the Town, The Sound of Music, Hello, Dolly!* (Regent's Park).

Opera credits include *The Handmaid's Tale* (Danish/Canadian/English National Opera), *The Marriage of Figaro* (English National Opera).

Peter is a founder member of FreelancersMakeTheatreWork

Tim Lutkin (Lighting Designer)

Tim is an Olivier Award-winning lighting designer. He is a graduate of the Guildhall School of Music & Drama and works as a guest lecturer at the school.

Recent productions include *Life of Pi, Back to the Future, Chimerica, Four Quartets, Fiddler on the Roof, Noises Off, Elf, Big, Quiz, The Full Monty, Impossible, The Girls, The Go-Between, Close to You, Strangers on a Train* (West End), *Under Milk Wood, Antony and Cleopatra, Salome, Les Blancs, Jack Absolute Flys Again* (Olivier Theatre), *A Number, Lungs, Present Laughter, The Crucible* (Old Vic), *Timon of Athens, The Rover, Candide* (RSC Swan Theatre), *All's Well That Ends Well* (Royal Shakespeare Theatre and national tour), *Macbeth, Chimerica* (Almeida).

For Walt Disney Imagineering: *The Lion King – Rhythm of The Pride Lands, Mickey & the Magician, Marvel Superheroes United, Frozen Celebration, Disney Junior Dream Factory* (Disneyland).

Tingying Dong (Sound Designer & Composer)

Ting trained at LAMDA and is a sound designer, composer and theatre maker. She co-founded Out of the Blue Theatre in 2020 with the aim of making bold, playful and accessible work.

Recent productions include *Peggy for You, Folk* (Hampstead Theatre), *A Christmas Carol* (Composer, Nottingham Playhouse/Alexandra Palace), *Two Billion Beats* (Orange Tree Theatre), *Antigone* (Storyhouse), *Klippies* (Young Vic), *The Sun, the Moon, and the Stars* (Theatre Royal Stratford East), *A Whole New World, Breathe* (Donmar Warehouse Online), *My Son's a Queer (But What Can You Do)* (Turbine Theatre), *ENG-ER-LAND* (Jermyn Street Theatre), *Bin Juice, Kraken, The First* (Vaults Festival), *We Like to Move It* (Ice and Fire), *Blood Orange* (Old Red Lion Theatre), *Jerker* (King's Head Theatre), *Chamber 404* (Camden People's Theatre), *Imaginarium* (online world tour), *Mr Kolpert, Yen, The Arsonists, Julius Caesar, Hamlet* (LAMDA). Radio includes *Humane*. Short films include *Medea/Worn, My Last Duchess*. Nominations include Off West End Award for Best Sound Design (*The Sun, the Moon, and the Stars, Jerker*).

Paul Arditti (Sound Design Mentor)

Theatre credits include *La Belle Sauvage, A Midsummer Night's Dream, Julius Caesar* and *Young Marx* (Bridge Theatre), *Caroline or Change* (Broadway, Chichester, Hampstead and West End), *The Inheritance* (Broadway – Tony Award nomination 2020/21, Drama Desk Award 2020; Young Vic and West End – Olivier Award nomination 2019), *This Is My Family* (Chichester Festival Theatre), *After Nora* (ITA Amsterdam), *Our Generation* and *Dick Whittington* (National Theatre), *The Jungle* (Young Vic, West End, New York and San Francisco), *Rutherford and Son, Pericles, Beginning, Macbeth, Absolute Hell* and *Amadeus* (National Theatre – Olivier Award nomination 2017).

Other awards include Olivier Award for *Saint Joan* (National Theatre), Tony, Drama Desk and Olivier Awards for *Billy Elliot the Musical*, Evening Standard Design Award for *Festen*, and Tony Award nominations for *Mary Stuart* and *One Man, Two Guvnors*.

Alice Hallifax (Design Associate)

Alice is a designer working across theatre, live music, exhibition and installation, who has worked on productions in the UK, Spain and Mexico. Alice has previously worked as design associate with Peter McKintosh on *The Sun, The Moon, and the Stars* and *Extinct* at Theatre Royal Stratford East. She has worked as a design assistant with Lizzie Clachan, Es Devlin, Rosie Elnile, Anna Fleischle, Peter McKintosh, Joanna Scotcher and Tom Scutt. Alice has run theatre workshops with Donmar Warehouse and Theatre Centre, as well as working as a scenic painter, prop maker and mould maker for large-scale productions including *Dreamgirls, The Ferryman* and *Harry Potter and the Cursed Child*.

Aaliyah McKay (Assistant Director)

Aaliyah is a British director and writer, whose family is of Caribbean and African descent. She has recently debuted her play *History on the Road* in two sold-out performances at the Cockpit Theatre. At the end of 2021, she was the assistant director on the part-gig, part-play *Typical Girls* at the Crucible Theatre. Aaliyah is set to release her short film which she partnered with Fully Focused Production company and Netflix to produce. Her work has also appeared in literary anthologies, magazines, music videos and screen publications. She also has many other film and theatre projects under way for 2022.

Bret Yount (Fight Director)

For Theatre Royal Stratford East: *Bubbly Black Girl Sheds Her Skin, Dangerous Lady, Shalom, Baby; Clockwork Orange – The Musical, The Graft, Two Women, Bad Blood Blues, The Harder They Come, Family Man, Gladiator Games, Bashment.*

Recent theatre credits include *The Glow, The Cane, Cyprus Avenue* (Royal Court), *Force Majeure, Teenage Dick, Appropriate, Europe* (Donmar Warehouse), *Spring Awakening, The Hunt, Dance Nation* (Almeida), *Much Ado About Nothing, The Magician's Elephant* (RSC), *The Normal Heart, Top Girls, St George and the Dragon* (National Theatre), *The Cherry Orchard, Hamlet* (Theatre Royal Windsor), *City of Angels* (Garrick Theatre), *The Son* (Kiln Theatre), *Nine Night* (National Theatre and Trafalgar Studios), *Caroline or Change* (Playhouse Theatre), *A Very Expensive Poison, Fanny & Alexander* (Old Vic), *Girl from the North Country* (Old Vic and West End).

Isabella Odoffin CDG (Casting Director)

Isabella's casting for theatre includes *The Collaboration, Klippies* and *In a Word* (Young Vic), *Small Island, All of Us, Manor, Three Sisters* and *'Master Harold'... and the Boys* (National Theatre), *J'Ouvert* (West End), *Antigone: The Burial at Thebes* (Lyric Hammersmith), *Moreno* (Theatre503), and *After the End, Extinct, The Sun, the Moon, and the Stars* and *Sucker Punch* (Theatre Royal Stratford East). TV and film includes *ear for eye, Boxing Day, I Used to Be Famous, Girl* and *Blue Story*, and as casting associate, *Mary Queen of Scots, The Favourite* and *Denial.*

STRATFORD EAST

Stratford East makes theatre both for, and inspired by, our community in Newham, East London. We continue the political and revolutionary ethos of our founder Joan Littlewood as a leading London theatre and civic hub for East London. We are driven by our art, inclusive and bold. We tell stories that provoke discourse about the world we live in and our place within it.

Stratford East is a producing theatre, built in 1884, in the heart of East London, situated a short walk from Stratford station. We have a proud history and an exciting future. We represent our culturally and socially diverse community in the work we make, the people we employ and our audiences and participants. We tell stories that are current, political and representative of London.

Alongside our work on stage, our Learning & Participation programme offers creative opportunities that are accessible and inclusive to all, with the aim to develop creative talent for people of every age.

After the End is presented as part of our reopening season, sponsored by Telford Homes.

www.stratfordeast.com

Theatre Royal Stratford East would like to thank all of our generous current supporters

MAJOR SUPPORTERS
The Dorfman Foundation
Barry & Ann Scrutton

LUMINAIRES GIVING CIRCLE
Grand Cru Consulting Ltd
Neil & Sarah Brener
Rosalind Riley & Tim Bull

INDIVIDUAL SUPPORTERS
Katie Channon
Sir Trevor & Lady Chinn
Dr Elizabeth Glyn
Stephen & Leila Hodge
Deborah Mattinson
Sir Ian McKellen
Joanna Vestey

JOAN LITTLEWOOD CIRCLE
The Daniel & Gaynor Harris Trust
Elizabeth & Derek Joseph
Rosalind Riley & Tim Bull

CRYSTAL MEMBERS
Andrew Cowan
Jane Fogg & Steve Edge
Patricia Hamzahee
Terry & Nicola Hitchcock
Nigel Farnall & Angelica Puscasu
Stephen & Angela Jordan

PEARL MEMBERS
Matt Clarson
Susan Fletcher
Patricia Hewitt
Christopher Hird
Andrew Hochhauser QC
Rt Hon Dame Margaret Hodge MP
Melanie J. Johnson
David & Marsha Kendall
Jean Lang
Derek Paget
Martin Pilgrim MBE
Peter Stafford Wilson
Danielle Whitton

HONEY MEMBERS
Katie Bradford
Mary Friel
Good Wolf People
Andrew Grenville
Adam MacDonald
Amar Patel
Bryan Raven
And all those who wish to remain anonymous

CORPORATE SUPPORTERS
Edwardian Hotels London
Fresh Wharf Estates Ltd.
MAC Cosmetics
Pinsent Masons LLP
Sky Arts
Swan Housing Association / NU Living
Telford Homes

TRUSTS AND FOUNDATIONS
The Austin and Hope Pilkington Trust
Belvedere Trust
The Boris Karloff Charitable Foundation
Bunbury Charitable Trust
Chapman Charitable Trust
Cockayne – Grants for the Arts
The Esmée Fairbairn Foundation
The Foyle Foundation
Garfield Weston Foundation
The Garrick Charitable Trust
The Gerald & Gail Ronson Family Foundation
The Golsoncott Foundation
Harold Hyam Wingate Foundation
Jack Petchey Foundation
The John Thaw Foundation
The J P Jacobs Charitable Trust
The Leche Trust
Linbury Trust
The London Community Foundation
Lyle's Local Fund
Mactaggart Third Fund
Noël Coward Foundation
Solo Trust
Theatres Trust
The Worshipful Company of Basketmakers

And all our Friends of Stratford East

To find out more about how you can support Stratford East, go to **www.stratfordeast.com/supportus**

For Theatre Royal Stratford East

Artistic Director Nadia Fall
Executive Director Eleanor Lang
PA to the Directors – Rosalind Burkett-Wenham
Artistic Associate Lisa Makin
Producer (Interim) David Adkin
Deputy Producer Lauren Hamilton
Digital Producer & Content Manager Sean Brooks
Sky Arts Associate Artists Mina Barber, Tabby Lamb
Agent for Change (Ramps on the Moon) Aisling Gallagher

PRODUCTION
Head of Production Jess Harwood
Head of Stage Dominic Kelly
Stage Deputy Daniel Steward
Head of Lighting Deanna Towli
Senior Technician Lighting & Video Jamie Haigh
Head of Sound Jeremy George
Production and Events Technician Ross Monteiro

ADMINISTRATION
General Manager (interim) Ali Rich
Planning Manager Georgina Easterbrook-Matthews
IT Systems Manager Stuart Saunders
Admin Assistant Maria Majewska
Admin Assistant (Trainee) Elliott Lawton

OPERATIONS
Head Building Duty Manager Charles Thomas
Building Duty Managers Semaicy Crabbe, Natalie Elliot, Judy Mackenzie, Morgan Malin, Jack Matthew, Daniel Roach-Williams
Project Manager Barry Cronin
Interim Operations Manager Carl Burgess

FINANCE
Finance Director Patrick Holzen
Finance Manager Colleen Francis
Finance Officer Sibhat Kesete
Finance Assistant Maryna Orlova

DEVELOPMENT
Development Director (interim) Jo Royce
Senior Development Manager (Corporate) Cat March
Development Assistant Andrew Choi
Marketing and Development Assistant (Trainee) Terrelle Iziren

LEARNING & PARTICIPATION
Head of Learning & Participation Flo Paul
Learning & Participation Manager Kirstin Shirling
Learning & Participation Manager (maternity cover) Pippa Atkinson
Learning Projects Manager Maya Pindar
Learning & Participation Coordinator Aaliyah Antoine
Learning & Participation Assistant (Trainee) Mascuud Dahir

MARKETING & SALES
Head of Marketing & Sales Katie Walker
Head of Marketing & Sales (maternity cover) Sarah Clark
Senior Marketing Manager Polly Cotran
Marketing Assistant Stephen Maydom
PR Agency Jo Allan PR
Audience Experience Manager Angela Frost
Box Office Supervisor Asha Bhatti, Amaryllis Courtney
Box Office Administrator Beryl Warner
Box Office Assistants Karina Ginola, Julie Lee

FRONT OF HOUSE
Front of House & Events Manager Jovan Jeremiah
Front of House Supervisors Carlos Byles, Rosie Christian, Alex Jarrett, Rosie Revan, Isabel Snowdon
Front of House Assistants Fatima Abukar, Tasnim Siddiqa Amin, Jermaine Anderson, Jade Benjamin, Emma Cavell King, Caoibhe Cochlain, Shifali Dunbar, Beth Easdown, Elsie Frangou, Sofia Genuise, Riva Grant, Isobel Hardcastle, Nia Jordan, Phoebe McDonnell, Michael Magero, Maria Majewska, Jack Matthew Charlotte Mak, Romae Mitchell, Chad Nickson, Natasha Nuthall, Rekkha Rajendran, Kaushik Reddy, Kelly Roberts, Abdul Sessay, Alfred Sibbons, Saleban Sulaiman, Sayful Taneem, Sophia Towli, Edward Webb, Daniel Roach-Williams,
Welcome Assistant (Trainee) Liam Burns, Kamran Islam

BAR
Bar Manager Esther Jacob
Bar Supervisors Alex Jarrett, Jack Matthew, Jayro Viapree, Chloe Wright
Bar Assistants Vanessa Anderson, Jess Enemokwu, Ariana Xenophontos
Bar Assistants (Trainee) Trishika Gujadhur, Lily Marie Lin

BUILDING & FACILITIES
Building and Facilities Manager Graeme Bright
Building Maintenance Technicians Mackie Constantine, Donald Mitchell
Domestic Assistants Kohinoor Akther Ali, Vida Osei Bowman, Abiodum Douglas, Belinda Lee Duffus, Vincent McGrath, Marjorie Walcott, Sydney Weise

PROFESSIONAL ADVISERS
Wrightsure Services Ltd Linda Potter
Sayer Vincent LLP Judith Miller

BOARD OF DIRECTORS
Chair Rt Hon Dame Margaret Hodge MP
Andrew Cowan, Cllr Joshua Garfield, Dr. Elizabeth Glyn, Patricia Hamzahee, Simon Haynes, Christopher Hird, Deborah Mattinson, Martin Pilgrim, Bryan Raven, Peter Wilson, Omar Bynon (Young Person Observer), Naomi Kerrigan Asress (Young Person Observer)

DEVELOPMENT BOARD
Chair Patricia Hamzahee
Professor Anne Bamford OBE, Dr. Neil Brener, Katie Channon, Dr. Elizabeth Glyn, The Rt. Hon Dame Margaret Hodge MBE, Derek Joseph, Baroness Denise Kingsmill CBE, Adam MacDonald, Tessa Matchett, Deborah Mattinson, Barry Scrutton, Julia Simpson

HONORARY COUNCIL
Derek Joseph, Jo Melville, Paul O'Leary, Mark Pritchard

After the End

Characters

Louise
Mark

Beginning

Mark *and* **Louise**. *A 1980s nuclear fallout shelter with a wheel-hatch in the ceiling, but in the present day. Bunks, table and chair, toilet area off and large metallic chest under the beds.*

Mark I'm carrying you. I can't find my way because the streets, the houses, the houses were gone, the buildings were rubble, so I couldn't be sure and I'm panicking, I'm scared, there's bodies everywhere and just, the only sound is things burning and I can see the cloud rising and there was fires inside the, the cloud, inside it, beautiful, just unbelievable just, and I got to the junction and I thought 'Is this the fucking junction?' there was no land marks, this is my fucking road and I've lived here for years but I didn't know if this was my fucking road even though I've lived here for years and I put you down next to this burnt lump, this body, charred, completely, like burnt wood, you know when it gets charred and it's cracked and you can break off a piece of charcoal, no skin, no clothes and her hands were almost ash, there was bits of her blowing away and I put you down next to this. And I'm clambering over the rubble trying to get higher to see if this is the fucking junction because if this isn't the fucking junction we're fucked, we're really fucked, the cloud is the only thing I can see above the fire and smoke and rubble and it's like it's rising with me and I'm thinking, okay, we've survived the blast, miracle, we've survived the fireball, miracle, but when that cloud starts to fall we're fucked, we're fucked, we're fucked unless we're in here.

And then I see next-door's . . . pattern on his drive, on his patio, it's a pattern, irregular sort of, it's a pattern but in the bit you walk on –

Louise Crazy paving.

Mark Yes, his crazy, yes, paving, his, yes, and I go back to you and I get there and the body is lifting itself up.

It's pushing itself up. It's trying to push itself, but it's crumbling. It's pushing itself up and its fingers are crumbling and it's pushing itself up on its palms but its palms are crumbling, but it's still pushing itself and a bit by the elbow breaks off and I can see meat and bone and I run. I run off.

I ran off and left you there.

Louise But you came back.

Mark Yes. I saw the crazy paving and I came back.

And I picked you up. And I brought you here.

Beat.

Louise Thank you.

Mark You're welcome.

Silence.

Louise But I'm starting my new job on Monday.

Mark Yeah, well that's –

I think that's probably . . .

Yeah, no.

* * *

Mark *is pulling out cans and supplies out of the metal chest, talking to* **Louise** *over his shoulder. She sits staring at him, lost in thought.*

Mark Chilli . . .

Chilli . . .

Chilli . . .

Baked beans, baked beans with sausages . . .

Chilli . . .

Tuna . . .

More tuna, with mayonnaise, I don't think that's very –

Chilli . . .

She gets up and comes over to him.

Louise I've got your number.

Beat.

Mark What?

Louise I wasn't leaving without, I mean I've got your number, Mark.

Mark Oh, I know.

Louise I've got your

Mark Oh, I know, I know

Louise Because I feel I didn't really . . . last night I didn't really

Mark Leaving-dos are always

Louise I didn't really – they are, yeah, leaving-dos are always –

Did I talk to you? Because . . .

Mark we talked

Louise We did, yeah, that's right, but, because I don't think I got the chance to talk to you properly last night

Mark Oh, no, no, you had lots, I mean you had lots, loads of people, you can't

Louise and I wasn't just gonna . . .

I'm saying I had your number, so it's not as if

Mark Oh God no.

Louise and I don't really remember

Mark no, no, I know, well, you were a bit

Louise I was but, I wasn't just never ever again or something, I mean

Mark No, we're friends, Jesus, no, I know

Louise Just so you know.

Mark Oh I do know, definitely.

Louise Do you?

Mark Definitely. We're friends, I mean, we're friends it's not just

Louise Exactly. Definitely.

Beat.

Did we row a little?

Mark No.

Louise Did we?

Mark No, no, well . . .

Louise We did, didn't we. God, not again.

Mark Well, yes, we did a little.

Louise (*laughing a little*) Jesus, sorry

Mark (*laughing with her*) no, no, it was just

Louise We're like kids or something, God, I'm sorry, was I an arsehole?

Mark no, honestly it was about nothing

Louise my memory is like in and out – was it about nothing? what was it about?

Mark Nothing.

Louise Really?

Mark it was about nothing, I mean so small, nothing at all

Louise Jesus, just arguing over nothing

Mark honestly don't worry

Louise like kids or something,

Mark and you'd had a few

Louise someone should smack us across the back of the legs

Mark so I know you didn't mean anything

Louise I really didn't, God I'm sorry

Mark because – no, don't apologise because I'm saying, I know you didn't mean

Louise I didn't.

Mark to be rude

Louise I wasn't rude.

Mark You called me a cunt.

Beat.

Louise That was rude.

Mark It was . . . a little.

Louise Sorry.

Mark It was a little

Louise Yeah, I know, I'm sorry, I really am, fucking hell, I really am

Mark Oh look, I don't think you meant it to be so

Louse when I have a few

Mark cruel

Louise Cruel?

Mark or harsh, I mean

Louise it was more like you're a cunt or something, like you just call someone a cunt and you don't really mean

Mark You remember?

Louise Pieces, I remember

Mark that's why I left the pub after you, to say

Louise I don't remember leaving, Jesus

Mark I wanted to say sorry, or, and that's when

Louise it happened?

Mark when it happened, yes, so we were lucky, when you think about it, we were lucky we rowed

Louise Rowing as a good thing?

Mark rowing as a good thing, yes, exactly. Because I think we were sheltered by, wall, a wall or something so –

Look, let's leave it, we need to get on. Imperative, so

Louise Exactly. Jesus Christ, yeah, exactly. But I'm just saying that I wasn't fucking off and not saying goodbye, because I have your number so I wasn't actually saying goodbye.

Mark I never feel like I'm saying goodbye to someone I really like.

Louise Exactly. That's exactly, that's how I feel.

Mark I'm really glad we talked about this.

He goes back to sorting.

Louise D'you want a hand?

Mark What?

Louise Sorting or . . .

Mark No it's fine I've . . .

Louise I could help

Mark got it all

Louise I could help or something.

Beat.

Mark Yeah. Yeah, okay. I'm, well I'm just sorting it into

Louise Rations?

Mark rations, yeah, it's rations, yeah, that's right, it's rations really.

Louise So it's days of the week?

Mark Yeah, and different foodstuffs, varied, variations. We're a bit short on food. We'll be fine. I mean there's enough for one comfortably and we can stretch, we can make it –

Louise My brother's dead.

D'you think my brother's –

Probably.

Don't feel

anything.

Pause.

Mark D'you think you're suppressing . . .

Louise No. I just don't feel anything.

Mark I cried.

Louise Did you?

Mark Sorry. I don't know why I said that, sorry, shit. Before you came round. Maybe relief at getting in out of, or something.

Louise maybe I'm concussed

Mark I don't think that affects your feelings.

Louise What was it?

She sits down and starts sorting with him.

Do you know?

Mark Terrorists. Probably.

It was small. It looked smaller than, I dunno, but I mean it must've, so . . .

Suitcase nuke.

Louise In a suitcase?

Mark No, no, they just

Louise How do you know it was in . . .?

Mark No, it wasn't, no, that's what they call them. You know, they're like a portable device that you set off yourself. That's why they say suitcase because like maybe you could carry one in

Louise Right. Why is there nothing on the radio?

Mark Could be anything.

Louise Like what?

Mark EMP.

Louise What's that?

Mark Electro magnetic pulse. Maybe. Knocks out all electrics in a certain area, maybe the masts, the transmitters

Louise Is that likely?

Mark No.

Beat.

We'll keep trying.

Louise Every three hours. That's what you said.

Mark Yeah. Every three

Louise I'm glad you know about this stuff, Mark.

Mark Ah, yeah. Well, you know. My shelter. So . . .

Louise So is this the menu for the next two weeks?

Mark Yes. Two weeks, yes.

Sorry. There's a lot of chilli.

Louise I like chilli. We can heat the shelter at the same time.

Mark Yeah.

Beat.

How?

Louise With all the farting.

Beat.

It's a joke.

Mark Oh yeah.

He laughs. She smiles. They carry on sorting. Suddenly he makes a farting noise. It is not funny, but she laughs anyway.

Louise You were right.

I mean all this. The shelter and –

Mark Louise –

Louise You were though, weren't you. We all took the piss. We laughed when you bought a flat with a shelter in the garden

Mark Christ, that doesn't matter now . . .

And that isn't, actually – I keep saying this – that isn't why I bought the flat

Louise I know

Mark I bought the flat because I like it and it's not too bad for transport and it happened to have an old shelter in the back

Louise Yeah, but you kept it.

Mark I kept it, yes, rather than tear out

Louise You kept it stocked up. In preparation –

Mark Which I kept stocked up because the world has gone fucking insane!

They sort.

Look, it wasn't about the shelter. It was because I got the shelter. I mean if it'd been someone else everyone'd be all 'Oh, isn't that great, isn't that funny' and all that old whatever, but because I get it

Louise Oh, come on.

Mark What?

Louise Oh, come on Mark, that's not true.

Mark It is. I mean I'm not being, it is, because if Francis had got it everyone'd think it was hilarious and really clever but because it's me

Louise Mark, it just seemed a bit

Mark What?

Louise a bit, well, paranoid.

Mark Paranoid? They've let off a nuclear bomb!

Louise I know, okay, I'm saying it seemed, at the time it seemed

Mark Well it *seemed* wrong, then, didn't it.

Louise That's what I'm saying, I'm saying you were right.

Mark Right but paranoid.

Louise Because, alright, but some of the things you say sometimes

Mark are right, were right, have turned out right.

Louise Okay, maybe they are, maybe . . .

Mark Well, who do you think did this then?

Louise I know, I'm saying –

Mark Well, I tell you what, whoever it was, you can bet your life they
had beards.

Louise Oh, Mark.

Mark Alright, sorry. No I mean, fair enough

Louise For Christ's sake

Mark Well, actually – now that we're at it, who do you think did this?

Louise I know, Mark, that's what I'm saying, I'm confused, I don't fucking know, but what I'm saying is

Mark What?

Beat.

Louise Look, there's all these people, right, who are just fucking saying I know what's best and do what I say or I'll or I'll shoot you in the head – on both sides, Mark, on both sides. And I just don't think that the best way to combat that is to start go round saying you do what I say or I'll fucking shoot you in the head.

Mark How do you fight, then?

Louise I don't –

Mark No, I'm interested.

Louise I don't know, Mark, I'm saying I'm confused, I'm saying this I what I believe and meanwhile my friends are either dead or screaming in agony or

Mark Because that's called burying your head in the sand. I'm sorry, but it is.

Louise Oh, for fuck's sake.

Mark Which is what I refused to do and which is what I was laughed at for.

Louise You weren't laughed at

Mark and you can sit there and criticise governments and politicians and whatever, and that's easy to do from pubs and trendy bars and sitting rooms, but at the end of the day you have to do something: the reality is tough, you have to close borders, imprison if you have to

Louise Jesus, Mark, you're sounding just a little bit fascist.

Mark And that is exactly . . . *That* is exactly the kind of comment and attitude

Louise *Look,* I don't mean –

Mark It's a war. We're at war, and just because the bombing hadn't started didn't mean it wasn't going to. And what do you want to do with that time, just sit and accept

Louise I know

Mark just wait there drinking, laughing, smoking, taking the piss

Louise I know, Mark, I'm saying

Mark Look at where we are!

Louise I'm saying I fucking know, for fuck's sake, I'm saying I fucking –

Mark Well don't start swearing at me all over again!

They sort in silence.

Louise I'm saying I know.

They sort.

Did you hurt your back?

Mark What?

Louise Did you hurt your back, Mark?

Mark Well, I think

Louise What?

Mark I think I grazed it

Louise Why didn't you tell me?

Mark I don't know, I –

Louise Let me see it. Let me see it!

He turns round and lifts his shirt at the back.

Jesus.

Mark It's nothing it's –

She touches it.

Ow!

Louise It looks like a burn

She goes to the chest, pulls out some ointment and bandages. She is at his back, starts treating him.

Is it radiation or . . .?

Mark Don't remember, I mean it was all, maybe it's a graze

Louise It's a burn.

Mark getting you in, it's a tight, maybe I grazed –

Louise It's a fucking burn, Mark.

It looks sore.

Mark It's a little –

Ow.

Yes, it is a little.

Louise You should've told me. You fucking tell me about things like this.

Mark Okay.

Louise You fucking tell me. I mean it, Mark, you fucking –

Mark Okay!

Pause.

Louise I want to get on. Okay?

Mark Okay.

She has finished. He turns around.

You know, I think we're going to be alright.

* * *

They lie on their bunks, wrapped up, cold.

Mark Cold.

Louise Yeah.

Beat.

Mark We have to save the gas. I'm not being bossy, Louise.

Louise Oh, I know.

Mark and the fumes are not too . . . so it's best

Louise We're fine like this.

Mark Yeah.

Yeah, fine like this.

Pause.

And sorry about the water as well

Louise Oh, no don't

Mark Again, I wasn't being

Louise Oh, I know, Mark

Mark bossy or, we just have to save

Louise I know you weren't, and I didn't mean

Mark because we can't really use it for

Louise I didn't mean to snap

Mark washing, you didn't snap.

Louise I did and I'm sorry.

Mark No, course you didn't.

Louise I mean drinking's more important.

Mark It is.

Maybe we could wash a little, though. Special occasions.

You didn't snap.

Silence.

Are you thinking about Francis?

Louise What?

Mark No, I mean, you know. Are you?

Louise Am I thinking about Francis?

Mark Because I just noticed in the pub –

Louise What?

Mark No, I mean I just noticed that you were friendly.

Louise Well, we're friends

Mark with him, oh no, I know, I mean . . . no, no, I'm just saying in case you wanted

Louise What?

Mark To talk. I thought you might want to talk about it. Or something.

Louise D'you think he's dead?

No answer.

I'm really glad you brought this flat, you know.

Mark Well. You know what we say in the reprographics department; tedious but lucrative.

Pause.

Are you thinking about Francis? Cos I mean if you wanted to talk –

Louise I'm thinking about my brother.

Mark Right.

D'you want to talk, or . . .

Louise No. Thank you.

Silence. He has an idea.

Mark They send the first two astronauts to Mars, right, and they're in their little – it's a man and a woman – they're in their little unit and it's a six-month flight to get there and they've been crammed into this capsule for six months together, a man and a woman, and they're there in their little unit and it's the first night and the heating's broken down and they're in their bunks freezing away, And she's on the top bunk and he's on the bottom bunk and they're both really cold and it's really quiet and they're both not saying anything – and after a while she says, 'I'm cold'. And he says, 'Yeah, me too'. And there's a silence and she leans over the bunk and says to him, 'Would you get me another blanket?', and he looks up at her and he says, 'You know, just for tonight, why don't we pretend like we're man and wife?' And she looks at him and she thinks and she says, 'Yeah. Okay. Just for tonight', and he says, 'Good. Now get your own damn blanket.'

Pause. He laughs a little to indicate it was a joke. Nothing.

It was a joke, it was . . .

Pause.

Shit. Sorry.

Fuck, sorry.

I'm sorry, Louise, it's, I wasn't, it's, I wasn't, I wasn't –

Louise Fucking hell, Mark.

Mark Oh my God I am so

Louise Jesus, where did you get that one?

Mark Louise, I am so, so . . . sorry, I am

Louise That's fucking terrible.

She starts laughing.

Mark I don't know why I said

Laughing harder.

Louise?

Louise That's the most stupid fucking, inappropriate

She can't stop laughing.

Mark Louise?

Louise You're so mental.

He doesn't know how to take this. Decides it's positive. Starts laughing as well.

Mark Yeah.

Yeah I know.

They are both laughing.

Fucking mental.

The laughter subsides. Silence.

I touched your breast.

Beat.

Louise What?

Mark By accident. I didn't mean to, it was, I was carrying you and your arm was hanging down and I realised where I was holding you and it was your breast.

I just wanted to say I'm sorry, and for it to be, well, open or

Louise Right.

Mark It wasn't anything like that, I just couldn't move my arm, because the cloud and . . . oh fuck, why am I saying this?

Louise Why are you saying this?

Mark I just wanted

Louise It's okay.

Mark shit, I just wanted

Louise Go to sleep, Mark.

Mark That's a good idea, sleep, yes. Good.

Silence.

Louise What do you think's out there? Now? I mean people and that. I mean d'you think there's people dying up there and –

There is, isn't there.

Mark Best not to think.

Louise No. No, sorry.

Mark Enough on our plates.

Louise Yeah. What's it going to be like after? I mean d'you think we'll all be like, will it be the end of things, will it be really military or, I mean will it be like checkpoints and things?

Mark Dunno.

Louise Will we just have to imprison people if we're suspicious of them or something, I mean will we all be bastards?

Mark I think we'll take . . . precautions.

Louise D'you think there's people searching?

Mark Not yet. Not for a long time yet.

Louise So people are just going to be lying up there? Dying. Screaming.

Beat.

Mark Best not think about out there. Got to concentrate on getting through. Hard enough in here, eh. We'll be fine, but . . . best not think about that, out there.

Silence. Another idea.

There are these three vets, right and one's – veterinary surgeons – and one's an – not like veterans, army or, but you probably know that – so one's an alcoholic, one's a drug addict and the other is addicted to pornography and when they get paid the first vet says to the second vet, 'Right, I've got this idea', he –

Beat. He looks over. She is crying. He immediately gets off his bunk and sits on the edge of hers. Puts his arm around her. She leans into him.

There, there.

There, there.

Middle

Louise I hate it.

Mark Well, you haven't –

Louise I fucking hate it.

Mark That's a bit

Louise I fucking

Mark negative.

Louise hate it.

Mark Why don't you just –

Louise because I fucking –

Mark You didn't let me finish my sentence, Louise!

Beat.

Louise Finish your sentence, then.

Mark Why don't you just try it?

Louise Because I fucking hate it.

Pause.

Mark We have to do something.

Louise Not that.

Mark We have to keep occupied, do things.

Louise Not Dungeons and fucking Dragons. Do you play that?

Mark No, when I was a kid –

Louise Do you dress up like a pixie or something?

Mark No, no, for God's sake, Louise, and I mean you don't dress up you just, look, I'm just, it's just a suggestion because we –

Louise Why haven't you got any other games?

Mark It was built in the eighties. It's an eighties game.

Louise You bought it two years ago, why aren't there games from other eras, why aren't there some nineties games?

Mark It seemed sort of – what nineties games?

Louise Pictionary.

Mark fitting, it sort of fitted with, you know, the, the

Louise Apocalyptic

Mark nuclear, because, no not, because when I was a kid

Louise You're not a kid.

Mark I know, but when –

Louise So you shouldn't be playing Dungeons and fucking Dragons.

Beat.

When can we try the radio?

Mark We tried it two hours ago.

Louise What I said was when can we –

Mark What's three minus two?

Louise One.

Mark You can try the radio in one hour then.

Louise I don't have a watch.

Mark I do, I can tell you.

Louise It's like time's turned off. Doesn't it bother you that there's nothing on the radio?

Mark I've made you a character, she's an elf called –

Louise I don't want to be a fucking elf!

Mark You could be a hobbit.

I think you're being negative.

Beat.

Yes. Yes, actually, it bothers me. But what am I going to do about it?

Beat.

Louise Sorry.

Mark It's only been three days

Louise Feels like three years.

Mark We have to look after each other.

Louise I know.

I know. I'm sorry, Mark.

Pause.

Mark When I was a kid I used to love it. Alright, yes, I'm admitting –

Escape or something, I don't . . .

I associate it with caravans. I've never been in a caravan. I think it was because a mate of mine used to go on holiday in a caravan and we never went on holiday and I always thought what it'd be like to be in a caravan. He'd always tell me stories of getting a girlfriend in this caravan –

Louise This isn't a caravan.

And I'm not your girlfriend.

Silence.

Mark Would you do it if Francis asked you?

Louise Oh, for God's sake

Mark No, I'm just wondering

Louise No you're not

Mark I am

Louse You're not because you're mental and that's a loaded question designed to feed into your paranoia about Francis.

Mark I don't have paranoia about Francis and this is, actually this is just like Jess's party.

Beat.

Louise Jess's party?

Mark Yes.

Louise Jess's party?

Mark Yes.

Louise Why are you bringing up Jess's party

Mark Because –

Louise What the fuck has Jess's party got to do with anything?

Mark Because at Jess's party, at Jess's party you were taking the piss and

Louise that was months ago, I mean do you ever let go of anything?

Mark taking the piss and belittling, you were –

Louise I was belittling?

Mark Yes, you were belittling me.

Louise At Jess's party, I was belittling you?

Mark Yes.

Louise What about you!

Mark What about me?

Beat.

Louise Mark, don't bring this out. Okay? Because we have to get on, but if you wanna bring this out . . .

Mark Let's bring it out

Louise because, I mean it, Mark, we have to get on

Mark I want to get on

Louise but if you wanna bring it out, if you do want to –

Mark I wanna bring it out, bring it right out, Louise.

Beat.

Louise You were acting like a freak.

Mark Me?

Louise Like we're all having a drink and a laugh and suddenly everything I say you're like jumping on, no you don't really think that, Louise, that's not you, Louise, why are you talking about *Love Island*, Louise

Mark You were being fake.

Louise Fake?

Mark You were pissed though, so I

Louise Fake? Who the fuck are you to decide if I'm fake or not?

Mark You weren't being you.

Louise You don't decide who I am, I decide

Mark We'd talked, when you first started, we'd talked about so many

Louise And I enjoyed those, I mean I really, we had some good

Mark Stuff that matters, like

Louise And I do, I like that, but who the fuck are you to decide who I am

Mark cloning and global, and now you're talking about this irrelevant

Louise I was just being normal, getting on with people –

Mark Upgrading.

Louise (*beat*) What?

Mark You were upgrading.

Louise Oh, for fuck's sake.

Mark No, it's fine, that's what happens, people want more, better friends and

Louise For fuck's sake!

Mark And you started it all with that stupid first impressions game.

Beat.

Louise Oh my God.

Mark What?

Louise Mark, is that what that was all about?

Mark Well, don't say it like it's petty.

Louise It is petty.

Mark You laughed

Louise Fucking hell.

Mark You laughed, Louise.

Louise Mark, you are mad.

Mark What's your first impression of Sarah, Louise – bit cheeky: what's your first impression of Gary, Louise – a good laugh

Louise I like you, Mark, but you are totally insane.

Mark what's your first impression of Francis, Louise – bit of a bastard, watch out for that one

Louise I'm in a bunker with an insane man.

Mark what's your first impression of Mark, Louise, and you just laughed.

Louise What's wrong with that?

Mark You laughed!

Louise It was a warm laugh.

Mark And everyone else laughed with you.

Louise I called Francis a bastard.

Mark A bastard is good, I would've liked bastard

Louise You're not a bastard

Mark but with me you just laughed

Louise Because I liked you and it was a warm

Mark and everyone else laughed as if we all knew what a prick –

Louise I mean is that what that all that was about?

Mark So tell me now then?

Beat.

Go on.

Tell me now. Tell me now what you thought when you first met me.

Pause. She comes close to him.

Louise Mark, I want you to know that I know exactly what I'm saying when I say this. I'm not telling you because I don't want to and because I don't have to, and I'm not playing Dungeons and Dragons because I don't want to and I don't have to. I really like you. I really think you're a good person and we had some good conversations, really good, but I think you are fucking mental and you're a control freak.

She goes and lies on her bunk. Silence.

Mark We have to play Dungeons and Dragons. It's important.

Louise?

It's very important.

Are you playing?

Louise No.

Pause.

Mark Well

I'm going

to have to insist.

Louise (*beat*) What?

Mark I'm,

you know, I'm going to have to insist.

Louise You're going to have to insist?

Mark Yes. Sorry.

Louise You're going to have to insist that I play Dungeons and Dragons?

Mark We have to, it's important that we keep occupied, this is actually a really important –

Louise How? How are you going to insist?

Mark I'm trying –

Louise No, I'm interested. How Mark?

Beat.

Mark This is my shelter.

I mean I've not said that before, cos I don't want you to feel . . .

Louise Are you going to kick me out?

Mark to feel, no, of course I'm not –

Louise Are you going to hit me?

Mark No, no of course I wouldn't, never, no –

Louise Are you going to starve me?

No answer.

Are you going to starve me?

No answer.

Mark, are you going to starve me?

Mark It's my food. Isn't it.

I want to do what's best for you. You know. Like when I carried you –

Louise Like when you touched my breast?

No answer.

This dream of yours. In the caravan. What happened after you played the game? What did the girlfriend do then?

We could play I spy.

Mark Okay, then.

Louise I spy with my little eye something beginning with 'N'.

Mark Nuclear fallout shelter.

Louise Yes.

Mark Look, Louise. I am –

I am going to have to insist.

Louise Go on then.

Fucking go on then.

You're gonna be really fucking sorry.

Mark What does that mean?

No answer.

Louise? What does that –?

I'm not bothered, I mean –

Louise?

* * *

Morning. Louise is brushing her teeth.

Mark I wasn't.

Louise You were.

Mark I wasn't!

Louise I don't care.

Mark But I wasn't –

Louise I don't care, Mark.

Mark But I wasn't.

Louise Then why was the bed shaking?

Beat.

Mark I was scratching.

Louise Really?

Mark Look I was, I was –

Louise Scratching the bishop?

Mark I was scratching!

Louise Look, I don't care.

Mark I do, I do care a lot. I would never do anything –

Louise Except deny me food.

Mark Is

is that why you're saying –

Louise No.

Mark because

Louise I said no.

Mark I mean it, Louise, because, that's, this is a serious, and I'm not denying –

Louise You are.

Mark I'm denying you some food, but I'm not denying you all food.

Louise A couple of mouthfuls of rice for a whole day?

Mark Well, that's up to you, look that's beside, I wasn't, I wasn't

Louise Look, just forget it, Mark, everyone likes the odd wank now and then.

Mark I wasn't! Is this something to do with

Louise Just do it in the toilet.

Mark Is it, Louise? The food or

Louise Didn't I just say no?

Pause.

Mark I wasn't.

Louise Well, forget it, then

Mark Yeah, but

Louise because if you weren't it's not a problem.

Mark Not 'if'; I wasn't, I wasn't –

Louise Well, good, then.

Mark No, because –

Louise Isn't it good?

Mark Yes, but –

Louise Good, then.

Mark Yeah, but –

Louise Alright, then.

Pause.

Mark Do you believe me?

Louise Yes, Mark, I believe you – you were scratching.

Mark You don't believe me.

Louise I don't give a shit, actually

Mark So you don't believe me.

Louise I'm agreeing. I'm agreeing with what you want me to say.

Mark Yeah, but you still think –

Louise No, I was mistaken, I was wrong.

Mark You don't think that. You don't believe me.

Beat.

This is how, this is where, this is where I am

Louise Just leave it, will you?

Mark Cos you're fucking so . . . you're so fucking . . .

So . . .

You're not quite as . . .

as you think, you know.

Louise Mark? I'm sorry.

Silence.

Mark You're not sorry.

You're not sorry, not for me. Not for me. What you think of me. The way you think of me . . .

He is crying.

Just some fucking . . .

Louise Mark?

Mark?

Mark I'm nothing, am I. Just a fucking little fucking . . .

He cannot speak.

Louise Mark? Oh, Jesus, look I'm sorry.

Mark? I am, I'm really sorry, I was just –

You're not giving me any food, you fucking –

Look, I'm sorry. I was just winding you up, I –

Mark *sorts himself out.*

Louise Mark, we're friends, we are, Mark, I'm just, it's just here. Being in here I feel . . . mental. I feel like my mind is being squashed. And I do

trust you.

Okay?

Okay, Mark?

Pause. He is looking at her.

Okay?

Mark You made me sick in the pub.

Louise (*beat*) What?

Mark You, in the pub, you looked so fucking stupid.

Louise Mark?

Mark Grinning at him like a

Louise What are you –

Mark like a fucking cat, all dopey eyed, you looked stupid.

Just fucking standing there gazing at him, gazing, just, you just, in front of everyone, *everyone*

Louise Mark . . .

Mark Francis, fucking Francis, like he's so clever, like, oh you're so fucking clever, Francis, you're so –

Beat.

Sometimes I used to look at Francis. Sometimes I used to look at him smiling there and I'd think to myself, 'The only reason you've got any of this is because I don't come up behind you with an ice-pick and shove it into the base of your skull. The only reason you're so wonderful is because I don't follow you home one evening and turn you into a paraplegic by stabbing you in the spine.'

Well, he's dead. So who's clever now?

* * *

Mark *cooking rice on a Calor gas burner.* **Louise** *entirely aware of the food, even when she is trying not to be.*

Mark . . . if you have a society, right, who is good, who is a good, a good

Louise Define good?

Mark I'm about to define, Louise, if you'd let me, I'm about to define. If you have, well, democracy for starters, you know, who feel that people, people can be free and, women for a start, who treat women like people, there's, and where you have rights and whatever, a legal system without corruption or where you can be equal

Louise Where's that then?

Mark and then you have these other – alright, fair enough, but I'm not saying perfection – you have these other societies that aren't like, that are repressive and dictatorships and where people are tortured

Louise Or starved.

Mark Alright, starved, they are, and then this first society, the good one, fair enough not perfect because that doesn't make sense, they have all the power, this first society has all the power but because of the way things are, all of our

Louise Decadence?

Mark Alright, I shouldn't've used that word, but yes, fuck it, decadence.

Louise Decadence.

Mark Yeah alright, I'm saying that fair enough

Louise The queers and the Blacks.

Mark No, don't because I'm not

Louise Go on.

Mark No, because I'm not, that's not

Louise Go on.

Mark Yeah, but no, because –

Alright we are a certain way, the people who live in that society

Louise The good society.

Mark Yeah, the good society, that society can't use its power to

Louise Force.

Mark Coerce, Louise, the societies, coerce and help

Louise Help?

Mark them to be

Louise Help?

Mark better than they have been and give people, the people within it rights.

But now . . .

Now that things have changed, we can see how stupid we've been

Louise by not dominating other countries.

Mark Well, yeah, but you don't have to put it like –

If you have power then you should use it. You have a responsibility to use it. For good.

Beat.

Louise Shall I tell you what I think?

He begins to dole out the rice onto two plates, a healthy portion for him, four dessert spoonfuls for her.

Mark Go on.

She stares.

Go on.

Louise I think . . .

I think, it's easy to say things. Alright, I'm admitting that. It's easy to have an opinion when no one's testing,

Mark Exactly.

Louise But now that people are dead . . . I mean I don't know what I feel, I mean my brother, I keep thinking about did he get home and is he okay and I know my friends, some of my friends are, and if I let it that can make me, I can get really fucking angry

Mark thank you, which is what I'm saying

Louise but that doesn't – hang on, Mark, hold on – I'm saying that doesn't affect what's right and wrong and maybe this is when it matters anyway or something. I mean just because some nutcase lets off a fucking bomb doesn't mean you should go around being a bastard and fucking with the brain of the entire world and saying right you do this or I'll kill you and your family and everyone you know. You either believe in something or you don't. Not just when you feel like it. When it's convenient.

He takes out an apple. Cuts a tiny slice off and puts it on the side of her plate. Puts the rest with his stuff.

I think,

He doles out the chilli, the entire contents on his plate, one spoon on her rice.

The only way people can destroy you is if you let them make you become something else.

He has finished doling out the food and now holds the plates. She stares at them.

Mark That's easy for you to say isn't it. 'Don't become something else.' 'Be yourself.' You're worth being.

You've got everything. People like you, have . . .

People want to be with you. When you walk into the pub people think, 'Oh great, Louise is here'. Your laugh, your smile. You know how to dress, you know what to say to people, what to think, what to believe. You've friends, good friends, real friends and you enjoy being with them and they love being with you. You don't sit there thinking, 'What the fuck am I going to say, these are the only friends I've got and I don't even know what to say to them, I'm making my own friends feel uncomfortable'. You laugh. You smile. And people look at your smile and they think that it's the best thing that they've ever seen. They think that it makes them look like chunks of coal, but they want to be near, even if it hurts them, even if it kills them and turns their souls into pieces of dust.

Puts food back into the box. Chains and padlocks it. Hold the plate out to her.

Besides. Everything's fucked. Out there. Isn't it.

He hands her the plate. She takes it and they sit down to eat in silence. She wolfs down every morsel, but when it is finished it is only enough food to remind her of how hungry she is. She stares at him eating his food, methodically. She stares. Suddenly she lunges for his food. He manages to get the plate on the floor and keep her from it. He pushes her away. They stand staring at each other. She goes for the food again, but again he pushes her away. Pause.

Louise Please.

Mark I'm just trying to do what's best.

* * *

They are playing Dungeons and Dragons. He reads.

Mark 'You come out of the forest and suddenly the keep is in front of you, like a ragged and ancient tooth on the hillside, jutting up into the night sky. It's covered in vines and ivy and bits of it are crumbling and the ancient path wends up to the portcullis. On either side of the portcullis are two forbidding statues of warriors, suggesting the ancient civilisation that once inhabited the keep, long since past. An eerie glow exudes from these statues bathing the entrance in a dull light and there are glints of moonlight –'

Louise What do you mean 'like a tooth'?

Mark That's what it looks like.

Louise It looks like a tooth?

Mark Yes.

Louise Like a tooth?

Mark It's not white, it's just the shape is

Louise Pointed?

Mark No, not . . . not a pointed, not a fang, I didn't say fang

Louise It's not just fangs that are

Mark Like a front tooth, a bottom front tooth.

Louise Right. I still don't get it.

Mark Get what?

Louise Why have they shaped it like a tooth?

Mark They haven't shaped it like a tooth, it's just a way of describing it.

Louise You said –

Mark That's just describing, it's an old tower, it's just this old tower

Louise Alright, I get it.

Mark it's an ancient tower that's sticking up

Louise I get it, alright.

Mark It's the ancient tower of an ancient civilisation long since deserted –

Louise Is it deserted?

Mark Well, that's what you have to find out.

Louise Can I find out by asking you?

Mark No, you have to go in –

Louise Alright, I go in.

Mark You can't just go in.

Louise You just

Mark Not just like that, Louise, you can't just

Louise Fucking hell, you just

Mark go in, because you have to be cautious and I haven't finished describing what you see!

Beat.

Louise Alright. Finish describing what I see.

Beat.

Mark '– and there are glints of moonlight on the ramparts.'

Louise Is that it?

Mark Yes.

Louise I go in.

Mark You can't just go in.

Louise Why not?

Mark Because it might be dangerous..

Louise Is it dangerous?

Mark That's what you have to find out.

Louise Can you just fucking tell me?

Mark No, because you have to

Louise This is shit.

Mark It's not shit.

It's not shit, Louise.

You have to figure out whether it's dangerous from what I tell you, from my description, from

Louise Alright.

Mark from what I've said

Louise Alright, alright!

Can I ask the pixie?

Mark (*beat*) She's an elf. There are no pixies in this game. Pixies are from children's fairy stories and this is not –

Louise Can I ask the elf?

Mark You can ask the elf.

Pause.

Louise Alright then.

Mark What?

Louise I ask the fucking elf!

Mark What, what do you ask her, what do you –

Louise I turn to the elf and say 'Is it dangerous?'

Mark She says . . . 'I don't know'

Louise Fucking hell . . .

Mark but she says, 'It wouldn't be too wise to walk into that light'.

Louise What does that mean?

Mark Look, Louise, I can't tell you every –

Louise Give me the description again.

Beat.

Mark 'You come out of the forest and suddenly the keep is in front of you, like a ragged and ancient tooth on the hillside, jutting up into the night sky. It's covered in vines and ivy and bits of it are crumbling and the ancient path wends up to the portcullis. On either side of the portcullis are two forbidding statues of warriors, suggesting the ancient civilisation that once inhabited the keep, long since past. An eerie glow exudes from these statues bathing the entrance in a dull light and there are glints of moonlight on the ramparts.'

Beat.

Louise This is what you used to dream about? Being in a caravan with this? A hobbit and a pixie and a tower shaped like a tooth?

Pause.

Mark She's an elf. She's an elf and you know she's an elf. You're just saying pixie because you want to sabotage the game. If you're not going to play it properly then you shouldn't –

Louise You're starving me into playing it!

Mark To help you, to look after you!

Louise To look after me?

Mark You say, 'Yeah, I'll play', but you can't just, just accept it and play, you have to call an elf a pixie just to remind me that you're better than me.

Louise Who the fuck –?

You're looking after me?

Mark Are you going to play it properly?

Beat.

Louise You're looking after me, Mark?

Mark Louise –

Louise Let's play.

Beat.

Mark Properly?

Louise Let's play.

Mark I want us to get on. Okay?

Beat.

Louise Give me the description again.

Mark 'You come out of the forest and suddenly the keep is in front of you, like a ragged and ancient tooth on the hillside, jutting up into the night sky. It's covered in vines and ivy and bits of it are crumbling and the ancient path wends up to the portcullis. On either side of the portcullis are two forbidding statues of warriors, suggesting the ancient civilisation that once inhabited the keep, long since past. An eerie glow exudes from these statues bathing the entrance in a dull light and there are glints of moonlight on the ramparts.'

Louise I walk forward, out of the forest

Mark I don't think that's –

Louise Can I do what I want?

Mark Yes, you can, you can

Louise I walk forward, out of the forest, very slowly,

Mark Ariel hisses at you to, to come back –

Louise very slowly, taking off my top

Mark (*beat*) What?

Louise I'm taking off my top and walking very slowly into the light.

Mark That's

Louise I pull my top over my head to reveal my bra.

Mark They wouldn't've had

Louise My undergarments, I pull my top over my head

Mark That's just stupid, Louise.

Louise to reveal my undergarments, and still I walk forward

Mark That's –

Louise And still I walk forward.

Mark (*beat*) The glints, you can see the glints moving on the rampart

Louise I carry on walking and drop my top to the ground,

Mark the glints are moving, Louise.

Louise and I begin to undo my belt

Mark Louise –

Louise Oops; my skirt has fallen into the dirt.

Mark You hear a shout in orcish from the ramparts and you suddenly realise that the glints were glints on the metal of the weapons of a troop of orcs.

Louise I walk forward very slowly into the light taking off my undergarments

Mark Louise –

Louise I pull it over my head, revealing my perfect elvish breasts

Mark You're a hobbit.

Louise revealing my perfect hobbitish breasts

Mark (*rolling a dice*) An orc arrow whistles past you.

Louise I'm naked now and I'm waving at the orcs

Mark Right, Ariel runs forward to defend –

Louise I hit her with my sword.

Mark What?

Louise In the face.

Mark (*rolling a dice*) You've killed her.

Louise I drop my sword and grab my tits

Mark They start firing

Louise and I wave my perfect elvish tits at them and

He suddenly scrumples up all the papers, throws them to the floor and turns to her. There is a fraction of a moment when violence seems possible. It passes.

Mark If you want to call me a cunt just call me a cunt.

Louise You're a cunt.

Pause. He sits down away from her. He pulls out an energy bar. Opens it. She watches.

Give me some of that.

He begins to eat. Slowly.

Mark.

Eats, taking his time.

You better give me some.

Nearly finished.

Mark!

Last bit.

You better give me some.

Raises it to his mouth.

I mean it, Mark, don't do that, because if you, if you do that, I mean it, because I'll really –

Puts it in his mouth. Chews. Swallows. She stares.

You fucking –

You fucking –

Pause. She stares, impotent. Walks away, furious. Calms.

Beat.

I remember now. I remember what I thought when I first met you.

Beat.

Mark What?

Louise Yeah. I just remembered.

Mark Don't say something just to get at me.

Louise No. This is true.

Mark Yeah, but don't say something just to –

Louise This is exactly what I thought.

Mark Louise, don't because –

Louise No, Mark, this is true.

Shall I tell you? Shall I tell you, Mark? Do you want to know?

Beat.

I thought, 'Ahhh'.

Pause.

Mark No, you didn't.

Louise I thought, 'Ahhh'.

Mark I don't care.

You didn't think, you're just saying –

I don't care.

Louise I thought, 'Ahhh. Look at him. Ahhh.'

Pause.

Mark I could really hurt you.

I could really hurt you.

Beat.

I could really hurt you.

Tens of thousands of corpses up there. People vaporised into shadows. No one knows you're here. I could really hurt you. If I was a bad person.

***

Louise *waking* **Mark**, *desperate.*

Louise Voices!

Mark What?

Louise Voices, Mark, I think I heard, outside there's

Mark What, what is, where?

Louise Mark?

Mark What?

Louise Out there, voices

Mark Voices?

Louise Yes, I heard

Mark (*getting out of bed*) No . . .

Louse I think so

Mark What out there?

Louise Yes, I mean there was this sound, I think, like on the hatch

Mark Are you sure?

Louise Well, I think so, I think . . . no, I'm not sure but I mean I was

Mark Were you sleeping?

Louise I don't think so, I don't think –

Mark Shh.

Louise I heard

Mark Shhhh, I want to listen.

They listen.

Louise It was this sound on the hatch

Mark Shhhh!

Louise like someone sitting on the –

Mark Louise!

They listen.

There's nothing.

Louise No.

Beat.

But I think there was, Mark.

Mark Well . . .

Louise I'm sure I wasn't

Mark I mean, down here we can't really hear

Louise I know, I know, but maybe

Mark four foot of earth, I mean

Louise I know, but there was a sound like someone sitting on, and then maybe it travelled

Mark What did?

Louise The voice, the sound, maybe the sound travelled down

Mark What did the voice say?

Louise What?

Mark What did the voice say?

Louise (*beat*) It was a boy.

Mark A boy?

Louise Yeah. There were boys.

Mark Boys? Out there?

Louise I'm sure I was awake, they were talking about clubbing and

Mark Clubbing?

Louise Yes.

Yes, I –

I don't think I was sleeping, I mean . . .

They were talking about clubbing and a girl called Chimge.

Mark Clubbing?

Louise Yes.

Mark And a girl called Chimge?

Louise Well . . .

I know it sounds, but I'm sure, Mark, I think I was

Mark It was a dream.

Louise Was it?

Mark Boys talking about clubbing and a girl called Chimge?

Beat.

Louise Let's bang on the hatch.

Mark What for?

Louise To get their attention.

Mark Who? There's no one out there.

Louise I know, but maybe, because if we could go out

Mark Stay away from the hatch.

Louise Mark, if we could go out

Mark That is the most vulnerable part of the whole shelter, everywhere else, four feet of earth. Stay away from the hatch. Go to bed.

He begins to get into bed. She waits, still unsure. Suddenly she rushes to the hatch, begins banging on it.

Louise HEY!

Mark Louise!

Louise HEY, IN HERE, HEY!

Mark Stop!

Louise HEY, HEY!

He drags her down.

Mark What the fuck are you doing?

Louise What if they're out there?

Mark Who, who? Who the fuck is out there?

Louise I know but

Mark All that is out there is a blanket of nuclear fallout, and if you open that hatch

Louise I'm not talking about opening

Mark you let in an avalanche of radioactive dust

Louise I know, I'm sorry, but what if it I wasn't dreaming?

Mark that will kill us – you mean what if there really were boys sitting out there in that nuclear fallout chatting about clubbing and a girl called Chimge?

Louise Well, if you say it like that, it sounds

Mark Are you okay?

Louise Am I okay?

Mark Have you had any other, I mean have you heard anything else?

Louise No.

Mark noises or voices?

Louise No.

Mark because –

Here, have some food.

Begins to get some food out.

Louise What?

Mark D'you want some . . . here, here look, I'm gonna give you

Louise Yes.

Mark Here.

He unchains the box, offers her an energy bar. She takes it.

Louise Thank you.

Begins eating before he can take it back. She stops. Stares at him.

Mark What?

Pause.

What?

Louise Why are you giving me food?

Beat.

Mark Because . . .

Louise What?

Mark You're hungry, you need –

Louise I've been hungry for the last four days, why now?

Mark Because . . .

things, you're hearing, you're . . .

hallucinating.

Louise Okay.

Pause.

Mark?

Mark Yes?

Louise Can I ask you something?

Mark Yes.

Louise And you not get angry?

Mark Depends what you ask.

Louise Will you promise?

Mark No, because it depends what you –

Louise What's out there?

Mark What's out there?

Louise Yes.

Mark What d'you mean? Rubble and . . .

Louise Really?

Mark fallout and . . . Yes, really – bodies you know. You know what's out there, you

Louise I don't.

Mark know what's . . .

Louise I don't know what's out there. I haven't seen it.

Pause.

Mark What? What are you –?

I mean are you saying –?

Louise?

Louise I don't want you to get angry, I'm just asking –

Mark Are you saying –?

Louise I'm just saying that, if there wasn't, if this *was*, or something, then this would be the moment. This would be the moment, Mark. To be honest. If that was the case.

Silence.

Mark Is that what you think of me?

Louise No.

But is it true?

Pause. He snatches the energy bar out of her hand.

Mark You fucking cunt.

Louise Sorry

Mark You fucking cunt, you fucking, fucking

Louise sorry, look I'm sorry, but

Mark after everything, everything I've

Louise don't get all, because I'm just

Mark done, everything, saving your, saving your fucking life, Louise!

Louise I'm really sorry, Mark, but answer my question.

Mark Answer your –

Louise Look, I'm not saying anything/ I'm just saying that if all this was –

He grabs her by the neck. Stares at her.

Mark, let go.

He doesn't.

Let go!

He doesn't. She tries prying his hand away, but it's no good.

Let fucking go, Mark!

She struggles more. Gives up.

Alright, I'm sorry, okay? I'm sorry, I'm really fucking sorry; only I had to, I mean I haven't seen, I'm just taking your –

Will you let go, please?

Mark, please?

Please!

He lets her go. Pause. They stare at each other. Suddenly she pushes him and heads for the hatch. He grabs her, throws her to the floor, twists her arm behind her back causing her to scream in pain and frustration. Grabs the chain.

What? What do you want?

Chains her ankle.

Alright, look you've made your point, I'm sorry, I'm really fucking sorry, now please let go.

Mark, please!

Mark I'm not having you open that hatch in the middle of the night. You wanna behave like an animal?

He wraps the chain around her neck. Padlocks it.

Louise Don't be fucking –

He slams his hand over her mouth.

Mark You shut up, you shut your filthy, fucking –

Beat. Takes his hand away.

No more words. Not from you. You don't deserve words.

Locks the other end of the chain to one of the bunks.

Right. This is what you want. Is it? This is what you're making me do. This is what you are making me do to you to help you. To help you, Louise, this is what I have to do to you to help you. No more nice.

Louise Mark –

Mark Why are you doing this to me?

End

She sits chained to her bunk, he sits at the table, wanking, talking to himself, muttering inaudible stuff. He stares deliberately at her, though it is as if she is not there. This goes on for some time. He comes. Cleans himself with the Dungeons and Dragons papers. Sits there panting, cock in hand. He looks up at her as if noticing her for the first time. Looks down. Begins to cry. Starts playing with himself. Gets hard. Starts wanking again, staring at her, still crying. She glares at nothing.

* * *

Mark *wakes up to find that* **Louise** *has a knife to his throat. It is the knife that he cut the apple with, a kitchen or hunting knife about six to eight inches long.*

Pause. She motions him out of the bed with the knife. He gets out of the bed. He is wearing only his underpants. They stand there, the knife to his throat. She indicates that he should sit on the floor. He does so. Pause. She is unsure of what to do next.

Mark We could have a conversation –

Beat.

We could –

God. This has gone a bit, you know, far and, hasn't it? And – I mean we're friendly, and friends and all this . . .

We could have a conversation, a talk and –

Louise Key.

Finds his trousers, gives her the key. Starts putting his trousers on.

No.

He stops. Beat. Puts them on the floor. She undoes the padlock, leaving the key in it, takes off the chain.

Food.

He goes to the chest, opens it. Pulls out a can of chilli, opens it, gives it to her. She eats, staring at him.

Cold.

Pause.

Said I'm cold.

He sets up the stove, turns it on. She eats, watching him. Finishes.

Water.

He passes her the water. She drinks. Lots.

Turn round.

Does so.

Sit on your hands.

Does so.

Look down. Close your eyes.

Does so. She takes off her top, keeping her bra on. Washes herself, dries herself, puts her top back on. Stands up. Looks at him. Stands close to him.

More.

Mark There's not much left, we have to be –

She touches his ear with the knife.

He opens another can of chilli, getting some on his finger. He is about to lick it off, when she grabs the hand. Raises it to her mouth, licks the chilli off, lets go. She takes the can of chilli. Eats, staring at him.

Louise Don't look at me.

He looks down.

Cunt.

Stupid cunt.

She eats.

Stand up.

He does so.

Close your eyes.

Does so.

Put your arms out.

Does so.

Up.

Does so.

Stand on one leg.

Does so.

Open your eyes.

Does so.

Sit.

Does so. She goes over to him. Drops a lump of chilli onto the floor. He stares at it.

Eat it.

Mark I'm not scared of you, I'm not –

Pause. He reaches out to the food.

Louise No. No hands.

Pause. He eats directly from the floor. He sits back up.

Stand.

Does so. She comes in, close.

I could really hurt you.

Beat.

I could really hurt you.

I could *really* hurt you.

Mark Louise, this isn't you, this isn't –

Louise Get your cock out.

Mark What?

Louise Get your cock out.

A moment. He stares at her.

Mark No.

Beat.

No. No, Louise.

Pause. He gets his cock out. She passes him some water.

Louise Wash it.

Washes it. She throws him a towel.

Dry it.

He dries it. She goes over to him. She places the blade of the knife under his cock. Pause.

Louise What's up there?

Mark What?

Louise Answer!

Mark Fallout, rubble –

Louise What about the boys?

Mark What boys?

Louise The boys I heard, what about –

Mark A dream, it was –

Louise I'm gonna cut it.

Mark Don't . . .

Louise I'm gonna cut it wide open and watch you bleed . . .

Mark Don't, please don't –

Louise Tell me!

Mark I have!

Louise Tell me the truth . . .

Mark It's the truth, Jesus, it's true, it's –

Louise Tell me the fucking truth!

Mark It is the truth . . . please, please!

He is crying.

She steps back. Stares at him – is he telling the truth?

Louise You're lying.

You're fucking lying.

She turns, heads towards the hatch – she is going to open it.

Mark Okay, okay, I'm lying, I'm fucking lying – okay.

But what if I'm not?

She stops. Stares at him.

Right, right, listen – what if I'm not and what if what I'm saying is actually true and

you do open that?

Because if you open that, Louise . . . we are both dead. Not maybe dead, not might die, but we will both definitely die, in fucking

agony, we will . . .

Beat. He controls himself. She hasn't moved – continues to stare at him.

What percentage of you thinks I'm lying? Is it what – fifty per cent? Sixty? Eighty even, I don't know, maybe it's even –

Louise Ninety per cent – ninety fucking five per cent –

Mark Okay, fine – ninety fucking five per cent, fine.

Our lives are in that other five per cent.

Because

alright, it's my life as well, right? You're not just killing you, you're taking my life and that's not, how is that even

fair or . . .

The tears come back, but quieter.

Louise Why should I believe you?

Mark I don't know . . .

because I'm scared, I don't know, I'm just so . . .

fucking scared

Tears. He seems genuinely scared. She stares at him.

Looks back at the hatch. Fuck.

Fuck!

She comes back in away from the hatch.

Louise Stop crying.

Stop fucking crying.

He doesn't. Not really.

Put the radio on.

A moment. He sorts himself out a little, puts the radio on.

That stays on. Alright?

He says nothing.

I can wait.

I've got everything. I've got the radio, I've got the knife, I've got everything.

I'll wait.

Put the chain on.

He doesn't move.

Mark No.

Louise Put –

Mark Alright, look, Louise; please don't make me put the chain on.

Louise Put it on.

Mark I won't do anything, please.

Louise Put it on.

Mark I'll be good, honestly, I won't –

Louise Put it on.

Mark I don't want to wear –

Louise Put. It. On.

Pause. He puts the chain around his neck. Picks up the padlock.

Mark Think the key's stuck

Louise What?

Mark I think it's jammed or

Louise It's not jammed

Mark no, hang on

Louise don't

Mark I'm just gonna

Breaks key under his foot.

Louise Don't –

Mark Broke.

Sorry. It . . . it just

broke.

She stares at him, furious – goes for him. He cowers, covering his head with his hands.

Sorry, sorry. Sorry, sorry, sorry, sorry . . .

Please?

Louise, it's Mark, it's Mark!

Please, please.

She stops. Moves back, shaken.

Thank you.

Thank you.

Pause.

Shitter.

* * *

Louise *is sitting over the stove, which has a pot on it. She pokes at the contents of the pot on it with her knife. The stove is unlit. She is wrapped in a blanket; he is not, shivering. He watches her. The radio spews static.*

Mark . . . and there was the time when your car broke down. D'you remember when your car broke down? We were in the Mitre and you were driving because you were off up to see your dad and you were sitting next to me, in the beer garden and we were squashed because there was a lot of us and you were squashed up against me, but it wasn't like that, but it was beautiful, and I was there with Pete and he was being alright, he wasn't being, Pete was being alright, for once, and the sun was going down and I was wondering what you were thinking. I was thinking, 'What is she thinking?' And I looked up and there was a star in the red, this bright star, and I thought that the world would be a perfect world if I could talk just to you. And then I thought maybe we were. Maybe on some level our souls were communicating, and I saw these beings of light, you know, the real us, not this corporeal, entwining around each other. And when you went, it was like dying and going down the tunnel and then being ripped back into this world by a defibrillator.

And then you came back. You just suddenly appeared and I heard myself saying, 'You can stay at mine' and you said, 'Can I?' and I said, 'Yeah. Yeah, of course.' And it was like the world had changed and everything on the planet was possible. It was a new world.

But you stayed with Mandy.

Silence. She tries some rice. Spits it out.

I told you.

Louise Shut up.

Mark I told you, it's inedible. It won't work. You need gas to cook rice.

Louise I'm soaking it.

Mark You can't soak it. It'll be sludge. You're cooking sludge.

Louise Shut up.

Mark I said we had to ration the gas, I said –

Louise Don't speak.

Mark There's days to go. Two, three days maybe.

Louise I can last two days

Mark Look at you. Jesus Christ, look at you, at what you've become.

Louise Look at you.

Mark Look at you. You can't live on uncooked rice-sludge.

Louise Shut your mouth.

Mark Okay, I'll shut up, I'll just shut up then, shall I.

Beat. She begins to scoop out the rice, try and make it into balls.

D'you remember softball? Softball? D'you remember softball? I remember softball. Everyone there, the whole company and I remember sitting under that tree with you, do you remember the tree, it was like a big, it was a big, and I wish I knew what type of tree it was, that's something I always mean to do is learn the names of trees, maybe some plants, I dunno, but we sat under that tree and this was probably only for, no more than, what? fifteen minutes? twenty at the most? and yes there was drink and yes you'd had a few and yes I'd been doing very well, a home run and I'd caught that, their first batter, I'd caught her out and yes, yes alright, all these things, yes, but we talked, we talked, Louise. D'you remember? We really talked. D'you remember? do you, Louise? we talked about the existence of life on other planets. And I was saying how they'd discovered methane on Mars and that this was probably the result of microbes producing the methane, d'you remember? and we talked about what happens if we discover life on the first planet we go to considering there's billions of galaxies, two hundred million stars in ours alone, that it would mean the universe was teeming with life, and it was like we were explorers, d'you remember? it was like we were explorers in ideas, it was like we were the first humans in an alien landscape and I could almost feel the tree growing under our backs and I turned to you and said, 'Aren't we lucky?' And you said, 'Yes'. 'Yes,' you said. And I thought, 'I love this woman, this woman, I love –'

The radio suddenly goes silent. Pause. **Louise** *goes over to it.*

Mark No radio.

Louise Stop talking.

She picks it up. Fiddles with it, but it is dead.

Mark Batteries. No radio.

Louise Stop. Talking.

Mark You can't last three days.

No food, no radio.

I can forgive you.

Louise Shut up.

Mark Look what you're doing to us. You can't last.

Louise Can.

Mark Can't.

Louise Can.

Mark Can't.

Louise Can.

Mark Can't, Louise, can't.

She goes back to the stove, but realising that the rice is useless she has nothing to do. Pause.

Then there was the fire drill. D'you remember that time they did the fire drill? There was the fire drill, d'you remember the fire drill, Louise? They called the fire drill and we all had to gather outside Tesco's and we started joking that this'd be a good time for the weekly shop, d'you remember that? I remember that, and there was the time when a dog came into the building, d'you remember when a dog came into the building? a stray dog and everyone stopped work and

She puts her hands over her ears.

watched, because I mean there was a dog in the building and we were saying, d'you remember, we were saying that Tony was probably going to ask it if it wanted to be a line manager and Tony was a little miffed at that and . . .

* * *

Mark *lies on his bunk fast asleep.* **Louise** *sits at the table, knife in hand, but her head is nodding. She almost falls asleep but at the last minute she wakes. Panics, looks at* **Mark***, but he is still asleep. She shakes her head, tries to rub the sleep from her eyes. She tries to stay awake but soon her head is nodding again. This time she nearly drops the knife. She gets up, walks around. Goes over to look at* **Mark***, see if he's really asleep. She goes to the hatch. Goes and sits on the cold floor. Changes position, keeping an eye on* **Mark***. Sits kneeling on the floor so that she can't sleep. Dozes out. Shakes her head. Gets up, goes over to* **Mark** *again, but he is still fast asleep. Goes back to her kneeling position on the floor. Her head nods.*

Lower. Lower.

Lower.

She is asleep.

The hand with the knife is in her lap.

She sleeps. Somehow this position has become tenable.

She sleeps.

She sleeps.

Mark *gets up silently and quickly, in one move, goes straight to her and grabs the knife from her hand. She recoils, instantly awake. He stands there in his underpants holding the knife. She backs away. They stare at each other. He has the knife at arms' length, furious. Long pause. He sags. Tries not to cry. She stares. The arm with the knife lowers, slowly. He is crying now, quietly, head bowed. She stares at him. Pause. He shuffles towards her, head lowered.*

She is frozen. He moves into her, puts his arms around her, crying, buries his face in her neck. She stands. They stay like that for a while. Slowly, she raises her arms, returning the hug, but.

Louise There

there.

They hug, both needing it.

They hug.

He begins to kiss her neck. She tries to pull away but he is clutching her hard.

Mark?

Mark?

His hand is on her breasts, in her hair, while he kisses her face through his tears. She struggles now, pushing hard at him. He lifts the knife to her neck and she freezes. He kisses her face, her mouth, still crying but pushing his groin up into her, against her.

She doesn't move.

Mark?

Mark My love. My darling.

Louise Mark?

Mark My beautiful darling, my beautiful Louise.

Louise Mark?

His hands are inside her clothes.

Mark, don't –

He pushes the knife against her neck and she freezes.

Mark My beautiful darling, my beautiful Louise.

He begins to undo her trousers, yanks them down. He is still crying. He forces her to the ground. He pulls off her trousers and knickers, kissing her stomach

My beautiful Louise, beautiful, beautiful

He performs oral sex on her, the knife now held directly above her stomach, the tip of the blade touching her skin. She stares at him. He comes back up, knife to her throat.

Louise Don't

Mark I love you.

Louise Don't

Mark My beautiful

Louise Don't

Mark Louise

He penetrates her. He moves with increasing desperation, still crying, occasionally saying, 'My beautiful Louise'. She waits for him to finish.

[AUTHOR'S NOTE: The above scene is what actually happened. But it does not have to be performed in full. Directors, producers and performers should take a view on what they are comfortable doing, and what they feel is right to show. What is important is to get the sense of what happened across, rather than to show every detail.]

* * *

Louise *is sorting herself out.*

Her clothing.

Mark *skulks in a corner.*

She finishes – goes over to the hatch. Looks up.

Decides against it. Has another idea. She comes back in, looks around – sees what she's looking for. The Dungeons and Dragons paper.

She grabs a sheet and a pencil, sits on the floor and starts scribbling things down.

Silence, apart from the sound of pencil on paper.

After a while he notices. Looks up at her. Watches her.

Mark What are you –

Beat.

What are you doing, are you . . .?

Are you writing?

What are you writing?

She doesn't answer, lost in what she's doing.

Louise? What are you writing?

A moment. Then . . .

Louise What you did.

Mark What?

Louise I'm writing what you did.

I'm writing it all down – everything you just did. I'm writing it all down so I've got it all.

Mark What I did? What did I . . .?

I didn't –

Beat.

What, is that supposed to scare, or bother, or something?

because that doesn't bother me, Louise.

I haven't done any –

Beat.

That doesn't bother me.

And what did I do, don't make it out to be all . . .

But she ignores him, absorbed in what she is doing, needing to get it all down.

He comes over. She doesn't stop writing.

I could just take that.

I can just fucking take that and I can rip it up, I can just fucking –

But she is not listening.

Suddenly he snatches the paper, steps back, holding it up and away from her.

She reaches for more paper, starts writing on that.

I can take that as well, I can take it all, I can . . .

But she just continues writing.

A moment. He looks at the paper in his hand.

What she has written. About him.

Why are you saying . . .?

Hold on, hold on, that's not –

Why are you saying that?

'your throat'? 'Hands on your . . .'?

Why are you saying . . .?

Louise Because that's what you did.

Mark Yeah, but you're making it sound –

She looks at him. A moment.

I mean, I'm not, that makes me sound –

She goes back to her writing.

He reads more.

Oh my God, 'legs –'

What, 'push your legs op–'?

But why are you making it sound like . . .

Louise It's what you did.

Mark But when you write it down, like a list, that makes it sound –

Louise It's what you did.

These are the things that you did.

And I'm writing them down so I've got it all.

She gets another piece of paper – continues writing.

He watches.

Mark So what, you just wanna hurt me now, is that . . .

Is that what you want, is that . . .

He makes a move towards her – she suddenly backs away, picking up an empty gas canister to use as a weapon. He stands staring at her.

Mark I fucking love you!

Doesn't that mean anything to you?

Louise No.

Mark I'm going to fucking kill you, Louise! I'm going to fucking kill you and then I'm gonna kill myself if you don't love me.

Louise Go on, then.

Mark I mean it!

Louise I'll smash your brains out with this.

Mark I'll win. You know I'll win.

Louise I don't care.

Mark Look at you! Look at what you're like now.

Just say you fucking love me!

Louise No.

He rushes her. She swings the canister, but he dodges the blow. She tries again, but it is too heavy to use as a weapon, and he manages to tear it out of her grasp. He grabs her by the throat, knife pulled back to stab her.

Mark Say it!

Louise No.

Mark Please!

Louise No.

Mark Louise!

Pulls the knife back to stab. Suddenly there is banging on the hatch. They stop. Listen. More banging, deliberate. They stare at each other. Pause.

The wheel starts to turn.

Say it.

Pause. The hatch opens, light floods in.

Say it, Louise.

Louise No.

Mark Please.

Louise No.

Mark Please.

Louise No.

Mark Please.

Louise No.

After the End

Private visiting room in a prison. **Mark** *sits at the table. There is a guard by the back wall.* **Louise** *enters,* **Mark** *stands. She is dressed up, but standing by the door, looking awkward, not quite knowing what to do. This goes on for some time. She seems to be waiting for the guard to say something, but he is silent.*

Mark You . . .

You can just sit if you want.

She sits. He sits.

Louise Hello.

Mark Hello.

Beat.

You look –

Beat.

Louise It smells in here.

Mark Does it?

Louise Yeah. Cleaning stuff, cheap cleaning stuff. I went to the toilet and washed my hands and it reminded me of this cheap hotel I stayed in in Turkey. I've never smelt that anywhere else. Straight back there. Five years. But it's like if I sniff my hands and try and be back there I can't. You know, it's like I can't

Mark I know

Louise catch it

Mark yeah, yeah I know

Louise with a memory or something

Mark that's funny with smells isn't it.

I don't notice that there's a smell, though.

Long pause.

Louise What's it like in here?

Mark Ah, you know.

Beat.

Louise No, what?

Mark Pretty shit.

It's prison.

Louise My solicitor said I shouldn't come.

Mark Yeah?

Louise She was dead against it.

Mark My counsellor thought it was a good idea.

Louise She thought it might compromise the case.

Mark I don't think it would –

Louise Are you getting counselling?

Mark Yeah, I'm –

Louise You're not a solicitor so you wouldn't know.

Mark No.

Louise Is it helping?

Is it helping you?

Mark I think so.

Yes.

Maybe.

It helps me come to terms with

what I –

Louise I fucked Francis.

Beat.

I was getting counselling. I stopped it. Didn't need it. I'm fine. She was very good but I felt sorry for her. She believed in forming a bond through empathy. Empathy as a two-way channel. So I would tell her what it felt like to find out that all your friends and your family and everyone you know had been incinerated in a nuclear attack and she'd tell me about missing out on sports day because her mother didn't believe in competitive sports. Embarrassing. Stopped going. Spare us both.

Mark How's Francis?

Louise He's good. He's going out with Sarah.

Mark Is he?

Louise Yeah.

Mark Really?

Louise Yeah.

Mark Sarah?

Louise Yeah.

Beat.

Mark When did that happen?

Louise That night we were all in the pub. Funny, eh. Then they sort of messed around for a month or so, you know, not sure sort of thing, but now . . .

Beat.

I don't think he wanted to fuck me. I think he was just being polite. I just thought it might help me, you know, find out some stuff. I scared the shit out of him actually. He looked terrified. I never really liked him that much. It just sort of became this thing, you know. You kept fucking talking about it.

Beat.

I had a hard time adjusting. First month or so. But I'm fine now.

Mark Why did you come here?

Louise How big is your cell.

Mark Ten by eight.

Louise Are there bars on the windows?

Mark No, glass it's sort of –

Louise D'you share it?

Mark No, I'm not very, they're worried that the others –

Louise What's the food like?

Mark It – it's not too bad.

Louise Really?

Mark Yeah, no, it's not great, but . . .

Louise It's not too bad, though?

Mark No, it's alright.

Louise I thought, 'I'll go in and ask him to kill himself'.

Beat.

I'm sitting there at home, last night, with this, with this cat in my lap and I thought, 'I'll go in there and I'll ask him to kill himself. That's what I'll do.' So I called my solicitor this morning and told her that I was going in after all and I called the prison service and they were very good, I thought it might take weeks, but they sorted out an appointment for today, which is quick, isn't it.

No answer.

I thought, 'I'll go in, I'll ask him to kill himself and he'll do it. He'll do what I ask. Because he was going to kill both of us anyway. No matter what his solicitor says, I know. I know.'

What do you do in here?

D'you get bored?

Do you read?

No answer.

Do you get telly?

Mark Yes.

Louise Yes? That's good.

Pause.

I find telly one of the most difficult things. Or I did when I was finding it difficult to adjust. My reactions to it are completely inappropriate. I'm at my mum's watching the news and this suicide bombing comes on and I start laughing, because seventy-six dead and they're all so serious.

I'm much better now.

Buying food was hard at first because I just kept buying it. I'd take stuff to the counter, hand over the money and almost run out of the shop, like I was stealing or something. This one time I was at Sarah's, there was a bunch of us and I saw this tin opener on the counter and I just put it in my pocket, and when I turned round they were all pretending they hadn't seen it happen and I wanted to fucking punch them.

Mark Louise –

Louise Don't

say

my fucking

name.

Beat.

I figured out how to make it better though. I just try and work out who I was and I act that. I just act that. It's getting easier. They said there would be a period of adjustment. It's getting much easier. The difficult thing is remembering. I find it hard to remember. And when I do I feel, like,

grief.

Mark I'm sorry.

Louise Are you?

Mark Yes.

Louise Well. That's alright then.

Beat.

So you're getting counselling?

Mark Yeah. Yes. I'm in group.

Louise In group?

Mark Yeah.

Louse Do you like it in group?

Mark Yeah. Yeah, I do.

Louise That's good.

Mark I want to apo –

Louise I think a lot about what makes people do things. What makes us behave in certain ways, you know. Every night I've been thinking about this. Trapped in whatever, behaviour, I dunno, cycles of violence or something and is it possible to break, these cycles, is it possible to break . . . And I'd be sitting there thinking about this and this cat, this gorgeous cat with no tail would come to my door, I'd have the back door open because the garden looks, and she'd be terrified at first, it looks beautiful it really does. So I bought some food for her and the first time she just sniffed at it and ran away, the moment I moved, you know, no sign of her for the rest of the night, and I'm thinking, reactions and responses, patterns, violence breeding violence, and the next night she's in a bit further and I'm looking at her tail thinking 'that's been cut off' and I don't think it was, I think she's a Manx, I think they're born without tails, and the next night she's further in and I'm beginning to get used to this, beginning to look forward to it. And the next night she's in and she's eating and from then on she's in every night; she's on my lap, she's following me around, she's waiting on the window ledge for me when I get home. And we sit there every night and I'm thinking behaviour and patterns and is it actually possible to break these patterns or whatever and she's eating and meowing to be let in. Every night. And one night she scratches me, out of the blue, cats, you know, just a vindictive cat-scratch, look:

Shows him.

see?

Mark Yeah.

Louise Just here.

Mark Yeah.

Beat.

Louise She knew she'd done wrong.

Took her three nights to get back into my lap. And I'm stroking her and thinking. Warm, delicate, you know. And I put my hands around her neck. And I squeeze. And I squeeze. Until her neck is about the thickness of a rope. And still I squeeze. And I'm sitting there – and this is last night – with this dead cat in my lap, and I thought I'd come in and see you.

And here I am.

Long pause.

I started the job.

Mark Did you?

Louise Yeah. A different one though. They gave my one away. But they made a new one for me.

Mark That's nice.

Louise Yeah.

Only I'm not quite sure what I'm supposed to do and they seem too embarrassed to tell me. I thought that it was just going to be like that for the first week, but it's been a month now and I don't seem any closer to knowing what I'm supposed to be doing.

D'you know what? if I'm honest, I don't seem to be that much closer to knowing what I'm supposed to be doing in general.

Long pause.

Mark When were you in Turkey?

Louise Five years ago.

Mark What was it like?

Louise Why? Are you thinking of going?

Mark No I just –

Louise Holidays, maybe?

Mark I'm just asking.

Louise Weekend away?

Mark I'm just asking, Louise.

Louise Why the fuck are you asking?

Mark Because you won't let me say what I want to say.

Louise It was very nice.

Beat.

It was very nice.

Beautiful actually. I wish I could smell that smell.

Beat.

I was going to bring you something but I didn't know whether I could.

Mark Yeah, you can, you just give it to, there's a place out there you give it to them and fill in a form.

Louise Right.

I thought grapes, but then I remembered that's a hospital.

Then I thought cake.

But then I remembered that's a joke.

Mark Yeah.

Louise Does anyone visit you?

Mark No.

My mum. Once.

Louise How is she?

Mark Not too good.

How's yours.

Louise Yeah.

I feel quite

alone.

Silence for a while.

Mark Are you

Are you going to ask me?

Louise What?

Mark What you came here to ask me?

Pause.

Louise Pamukkale. That was the place, in Turkey, that was the place, just remembered, we stayed, it was . . .

Haven't said that word in years, funny how . . .

how you don't lose a word, or . . .

Beat.

It was beautiful.

Pause.

Mark?

Mark Yes?

Beat.

Louise Do I look like me?

Beat.

Mark Yes.

You do.

Louise Do I?

Mark Yes.

Louise Honestly?

Mark Yes, honestly.

Louise Because I just need –

I was wondering, you know, I . . .

whether

I just need to know –

Honestly?

Mark Yeah.

Pause.

Louise I thought I did.

That's good.

That's good.

Silence.

Suddenly she gets up.

I think I'll go.

He gets up.

Better go.

Mark Okay.

Louise S'long way back.

Mark Yeah, yeah.

Beat.

Louise If I come again should I bring cigarettes?

Mark I don't smoke.

Louise Yeah, but you know; prison.

Mark Just bring chocolate.

Louise Right.

Over.